I Think I'm Ready to See Frank Ocean

Shayla Lawson

saturnalia books

Distributed by University Press of New England
Hanover and London

Saturnalia Books
105 Woodside Rd.
Ardmore, PA 19003
info@saturnaliabooks.com

ISBN: 978-0-9899797-8-8
Library of Congress Control Number: 2017957998

Book Design by Robin Vuchnich
Printing by McNaughton & Gunn
Cover Art: Frank Ocean illustration by Jack Hughes. Reprinted courtesy of The Village Voice.

Author Photo: Shayla Lawson

Distributed by:
University Press of New England
1 Court Street
Lebanon, NH 03766
800-421-1561

Thank you to Eaton Lambert, Shannon Slocum, Sarah Blake, Chet'la Sebree, Ross Gay, Richard Cecil, Yasmin Belkhyr, Peter Kispert, Henry Israeli, Rebecca Lauren, Christopher Salerno, Colin Walker, Joshua Johnston, Paul Asta, Michael Mlekoday, Allen Hunter, Sean Sanford, Justin Wade, Rosa Bounds, Jared Robinson, Nana Boateng, Coleman Stevenson, Erin Keane, Laura Luitje, Patrick Kayser, Samiya Bashir, D.A. Carter, Jared Williams, Brian McQueen, Dan Bernitt, & the MacDowell Colony—without you these poems may not have ever made music.

Many thanks to the journals: *Salon; Wildness; Zocalo Public Square; Connotation Press; Forklift, OH; Painted Bride Quarterly; Geometry; Opossum; Nice Cage; The Auburn Avenue; Witness; The Offing; Hobart; Barrelhouse; Guernica; Winter Tangerine Review; pluck!; Drunken Boat;* and the anthologies *It Was Written: Poetry Inspired by Hip Hop* & *Black Bone: 25 Years of the Affrilachian Poets* for publishing early versions of poems that appear in this book.

Table of Contents

BLOND(e)

channel(ed), ORANGE

START

The name of how music plays / often means what it is: A record—a witness; a cassette—a small blank conch. I rewind / this track / every time I want to feel ice / shaking off wings—I say "I want to see Paris" & mean I have never / made love. I remember / the laughter, the years / of blissful know-nothing / enchanté as love scrawled / in Sharpie / on compact discs: a mixtape—a shot / to the heart. / The Ocean—a Lincoln lost / on its way pacific. Carefully clicking on the sea / change of its own composition—the bullet / pop; the clip of the deck; the crack / of a knee's crease pulling from leather / bucket seats. & as I tune / to the east, the Ocean plays, stations westward; envisions / the gleam of ward rooftops is actually coast.

THINKIN BOUT YOU

Never let an ocean love you. He'll take
an eternity to do so. Like when Moses

asked of the-one-true-God, "Who
should I say comes for the sons

of Israel?" & God said, "Tell them
—I SHALL PROVE TO BE

WHAT I SHALL PROVE
TO BE," which is better than I-Am

-What-I-Am because I could say, "Prove it"
for, I am what I am as well. I wonder

if the ocean will get any older the way
I wonder about humanity. Would it

feel slick as cool new paint on the fender
of a wave headed off to join the tide? *A tornado*

lifting its brow from under a ball cap
scurrying around the shag rug, pushing

bed linens to wall posters, kicking away
shoes. No (it *usually doesn't rain*

it torrents). I wonder when Frank sees
the ocean if he feels naked as it is & becomes

a bit ashamed. When the ocean sees the same
does it too curl its large toe under the lining

of a tube sock & shy away from reflection?
Does it think about the *mess it made*

—songs floating on the bed of a one
room studio apartment? O Christopher

O Francis-I-Have-Not felt
so tuned to the earth it spirals

to the tilt of a bass clef
to the sun, since singing backup

for Al Green through the air ducts
of a Piccadilly Circus vintage shop.

How else do you mend a broken heart?
Eyeliner, sequin gowns, lapis lazuli.

How does the rain stop? (It doesn't.)
Even my mother in her arid

rock / gods—feathered hats, Sly
Stone, & Jagger—beat the desert-

dry July of *Southern California*
asking, 'What makes the world

go round' of Al-Green-as-always.
My eyes don't shed tears

but boy they bawl / just thinkin bout
it. None of us know what makes

the world go round anymore
than we know if love is

the deflated beach/-ball we keep
blowing up & putting our ear against

just to hear The Ocean inside:
every crush, a cymbal crash

every tear heavy as the sea Moses held back
with a staff. He sees his face in the eye of

a whale & isn't scared. Never
let an ocean love you. He will only take *forever*.

SIERRA LEONE

How often
I think
of her
pink skies
—the cut
& stench
of her
vacant
clitoris
close to
the burning
of her
father's hair
melting into
dust as
she watches
soldiers light
& impale
him. She
reeks of
menarche; open
anew
every time
she's bled.

Sierra
Leone
she's been
alone alone
alone she's

been a
-lonely; Daddy's
little *girl*:
baby no
longer. This
incision meant
to keep
her whole
only leaves
her empty.
A new
country in
which she
refugees; *baby*
girl on
her hip
I lift
from her
weight.
The infant
gums my
covered nipple.
I hug
& I pray
this is
the only
way she
will ever
be touched.

Sometimes
I look
at the

sky &
think God
has abandoned
us. The
sunset first
evidence he
has cleared
out &
left. *No*
I don't
live in
Denver. I
live in
verse &
verse &
scripture &

Sierra
Leone

cradling her
baby / girl:
a blood-
red meridian
(like a flood).

SWEET LIFE

The best song wasn't the single, but you weren't either.
                                    –Frank Ocean

Southern-bred good
looks & a penchant for brown

girls, a *paradise* of blue
-grass, dirt deep-

rooted. My maypole of new
green, bright in the bud. Making

out on your father's couch, *surreal*
art & tea roses, a parade of ivy.

Past the picket fences & our club
-house pool, the summer bent

its broken script on water:
escape in *wave* & pigment.

But I couldn't. I lost
an ocean of heartache in each

kiss, the crest of your tongue
the clamor of the mechanic

sprinkler system, porch swings
slivered with heat. Never mind

I shared you with peaches—other
dark-skinned débutantes—color

enough to keep the neighbors
nervous. You tasted

sweet. *The best song
wasn't the single, but you*

necking
the tops of topiaries

lawn blaring 808s & bass
guitars to vibrating

chrysanthemums; tuning
the radio to a noise next-door

lays to waste with weed
-cutters; a grapevine

wild in our fresh
sweet youth. I mean

*why see the world
when you've got the* beast

—a bevvy
of limbs hemlocked

in your backyard, a pair
of post-racial

pruning sheers
—an *ape-shit* suburb.

SUPER RICH KIDS

After Earl Sweatshirt

Too many toasties cut in quarters for Subway.
Too many indemnity claims at Allstate.
The sky clocking round *too much*;
Half-dollars just ain't down *enough*.
Too many key-bored schemes of my odd future;
Remixes of thwarted love toned grapheme-synesthesia.
Super rich kids string laces from loose ends;
Super rich kid with marginal dividends.

...

Too many sheep dreams when I electric blog.
Too many 'keeping up' with every Jones they saw.
But I'm treading waves because;
The stars shine; my eyes tear up.
I've written ubiquitous vocalists one-thousand trackses.
The best advice that I ever got was, 'Pay your taxes.'
Super rich kid with superfluous dividends.
Super rich kids string laces from *loose ends*.

...

PILOT JONES

Just like the hurricane, Lonny
understands destruction. The force
a body swallows to remember itself

mortal (remember, you too are smoke).
A woman loots across the Louisiana
heat & unbuttons right in front of him

from *lawn* sprinkler to downpour. She
takes her index finger along her navel
slides her hands soaking across his

lips. "Katrina," he utters as her wreckage
bows the floorboards of his college
years, drenches his sneakers in silt.

The dealer & the stoner, the rage
of her waters his song with falsetto.
Louisiana, & the Ocean is still a babe

who has not taken on the tidal
a litany of deluge: Four hundred thousand
heartbreaks. All carried away like the flood

he would become. Katrina:
what she don't drain she baptizes
in the trace of burnt grass that follows

all young men, one way or the other: *High
& dry*. But little *baby*, don't cry. Lonny gets
by even in the levee's descent. Katrina

rescinds & he becomes The Ocean, channels
orange—the absence of blue—like *the sky
up above* has *never seen* the gulf.

PYRAMIDS

(Adonai,
Adonai, my
Lord.) The Jesus
I know died on a pole. He
was not a God; he did not want to

be. He told
the thief hanging
beside him "Welcome
to Paradise," but all the man
could see were *pyramids—cheetahs*

thrashing
their tails
like a wild
mob. I mean, what's
the difference between the King

of
All Kings
& the Lord of Man
& the god of your Last Will
& Testament? In my favorite stripper

fantasy
Cleopatra
wears spots. She
scaffolds around you like
a vortex. I lick her cheetah paws

lap
dance into
your arms like
the baddest deity
of your dreams. *The way*

you
say my name
in bed. You curse
every god you have
ever met. What's the

difference
between a
woman set *loose*
& a *loose* woman
& a woman who crowns

herself
Pharaoh
of a country
that is not hers?
The Jesus I know is not

the kind
of insurgent
Jerusalem expects
after all that time building
the pyramids. I wonder why

if we
are gods
ourselves, we
revival—shout the
names of men en masse

worshipped
only out necessity.
I am the god you hail
from champagne flutes to
baptism. I disrobe all my God

-given
parts. I crumble.
I fall. I know. I love
only you & you & you
& *working* out *the pyramid*
-scheme: my own toned glory.

WHITE

sounded like houndsteeth / crashing into one another on rain-coats / eclectic as the sound of rain-water / in Costa Rica: pst pst pst pst / or in Texas: yes. The scent of shaving cream the scent of unwashed teeth & I felt so / I felt so / so lightly full of openings / so much / stiffness jostling like locks / between train cars. Not like these borders / we / wish to beseech. You turned to me & said: I can't put my finger / on it but I might as well / stick a thumbtack in that map / & cloud / string you along through every fog. This is how I know the rain / in Panama: says tsk tsk tsk tsk / & in Jamaica reminded / me of lit transparent / plastic / parkas we pulled from the first / aid kit when the sky / poured like a lift of / tropical birds. The car was rented. Or we didn't have a car / we rode / the one-eyed mammal. The bus: / sauntered lazily as a dew bead—he looked— he looked at us. He percussed / the books of his reflections for two / creatures tall & not quite / lean enough to eat like the rock-/ sands of Greece that pill into our skins the shape / of shadows behind cat-hairs. And I do not / write about you for you / are not washed out.

BAD RELIGION

Many things are oceans: the River
Styx, the Thames, & Lonny

flooding into a *rush hour* taxi cab, pushing
salt crust from his face, gut-wrenched

coral—twisting in his sea bed. Where
are you going? Anywhere that doesn't

hurt. He squints into the bright
wind as if light / sees him

for the first time & comes out a chorus
organ of tongue & sacrament. Let's

be Frank, he sings the force
of what it feels like to pray. *Allāhu*

Akbar—God is great. God is often
a language no one understands. Between us

a language barrier. *Allāhu Akbar*—Frank
hears the cabbie utter as a curse, but

the only thing this rented maharishi
demands to offer is supplication: prayer

for the Styx, prayer for the eaten, prayer
for the Ocean itself. For the days

he prayed to you like God, as I did. Allāhu
—God is. Akbar—is greatness thrust upon men

when we love them. Allāhu—for the God
they compete with. *Bo Bo*—the boy is

breaking up / like static, *'Bo Bo you need'*
says the *taxi driver, 'But boy you need '*

love equal to the God
working within yourself.

Drinking the Kool-Aid
is a phrase only

Americans use. No one ingests it
anywhere else. No one brings Styrofoam

to their lips in atonement. But, "O God"
O God, is everywhere. God is a neon

phrase. A testimony to the incandescent
sound of gnats crashing

upon the windshield of this slow-motion
hornet—this filament. How often Frank

prayed to you instead of God like
I did. What man brings forth

is night—but, what are we to do
with the light,   Light?

PINK MATTER

Four years after our wedding & Frank
oceans in us a salmon run: anadromous. Up-
stairs, you play *Pink*
Matter on repeat while I tap the keys
on the bed, on the laptop, on the floor
beneath—in this way we cease
to *matter*. The *pink* humming
between us, a telltale
tongue. Sometimes we make love.
Sometimes we imagine the other
cut into pieces, the parts we no longer
appreciate excised like rot fruit. I perspire
into the lining of the house, peach
split & nectar. Dissection, the drone of
endless *pink & pleasure*
   pleasure
   pleasure
you are giving & taking
away from me. You play the song
on repeat as if you know we are already past
tense, & we are not in rooms but ripples
of our former selves reflecting
into the Ocean. Sometimes we make
love. Sometimes we sex like we are swimming
on gravel beds, spawning the great grey
last of what we hate
in ourselves made flesh
in each other. We don't ask 'what
's the *matter?*' *Matter* is all
that is left—a remnant of body:

Androgyne. Man & Woman. With you
I am mostly *purple*. When you go, I take
inventory of all my *pink* & turn out
blue

                              (*used to be my favorite
                    color. Now I ain't got no choice*).

FORREST GUMP

you called me your Jenny.
I asked if that made me
the whore & you the idiot
which you didn't find funny.

We could rap for hours:
into tape recorders, over
your mother's kitchen island
in bowls of shito & cod

fish & rice. You call me
out when years later I come
home & ask, "if someone
will pass the pepper

please." You threaten not
to let me eat it, as if
I had forgotten the taste
of lightning, or ash

or you—or your Ghanaian
mother's nipple
which I sometimes believe
she used to feed us

both. My mother
begged yours not to
wash us in the same
bath & she did not

listen, cleansing the cruel
Puritanical stench
of our Middle-
American upbringing

in sponges & bubble soap.
I think about your hair, scented
aniseed. The bright pink bud
of your still-fresh circumcision;

how, your Ghanaian father
tried to hide our nakedness
from each other—as we grew
older, together & too unashamed

—your mother called this
wanderlust "showing off."
Sometimes you were the whore.
I fly in to visit your parents.

You show up high, driving
a black BMW, raiding the French
door refrigerator for Swiss
cheese & grass-fed milk. You lift

your *lips* to the carton & catch
me watching your arm flex
into a murder of crows, a dozen
shattered shingles.

You drive back to Baltimore
for your girlfriend
through the deer
-scattered forest of the rest

of this country. I writhe
in the dark in your parents'
guest room, lying
naked as a question

while I fall asleep. Sometimes I was
the idiot. My phone is vibrating
at three am, "Are-you-still-up?"
although it's been months

since I last saw you & I almost
think you are going to say we've lost
someone. Still, at three am
what could a beautiful man have

to say that isn't bad news?
We talk about the music
you still skin around
your *fingertips*—our

Middle-American heartbreak
—a reason to turn this story
to a record. The wilderness
that fills everything else.

Back together at your mother & father's
Ghanaian dwelling, we toast
the blessings of a Middle
-American upbringing

with Australian Shiraz, two imported
Ivy League cousins. I touch
your perfect arm branded
in a sleeve of ink:

the stint you did upstate.
Perhaps you knew no better way
to assimilate than to be shackled
by this country's past—its Native

Son—black boy cuffed
in the suit of a man, uncertain
what that means, yet
my fingertips & my lips still

burn, these new lashes
on your arm like the sting
from *cigarettes. Forrest Gump*
you know, a picture

of our first kiss *still* rests
on the ledge in your parents'
living room. We are at the Renaissance
Fair. You are carrying a sword

& I wear a princess crown.
Sometimes we were the idiots
who believed the future was just
the past made: naked: whole: again.

ULTRA, nostalgic

STREET FIGHTER

You would have been my first / kiss if you didn't always / beat me in Street Fighter. I wanted to be / Chun-Li—sometimes Guile (for the back story)— or Dhalsim: I'd call myself a pacifist / KO-ing heavyweights with my elastic limbs. I expelled most of grammar / school in an arcade attached to the Regal Cinema 6 at the mall adults stopped going to / or running boys down wild during recess trying / to punch them in the face. Even when I had your blush-wet cheek / pinned to the cinnabar dew-on-asphalt, I only wanted you to understand / what I heard behind my eyelids: the color Goethe attributes to the {energetic: crude: robust}. I paint the town— yellow red—love is the game / of the {young: nostalgic: grotesque}. My lips spare no vermillion. I hadouken Ryu's gee back to his tape deck.

STRAWBERRY SWING

I listen to the guns. They clear
the ground of all its color
& I flirt. I kiss you in the grove
too quickly. I swing through

your undress the words that "black
lives ..." I do not know
how to ask you to
love me yet. For everyone of us

I see die, I take you in
with all my air. It hurts.
I let you go just to keep breathing.
I have one transcendental

hope that God is erasing our kind
from the dirt. In the paradise
in the *spaceship* of His own
making, we will wake

to a field of clean dark
faces. Right now, I fear my own
mortality. I see the news. I might die
with you. I hope it is

the *atom bomb* that lifts the bright
pink off our mouths; we are nothing
to each other as our imprint
leaves the smoke. I do not want to be

the chalk-drawn street, the square
outline of our arms turned to one
smudge while we grow
cold in the blood like the *strawberries*

we trowel between our mouths. We play,
we only practice when we kiss each other.
But I am not pretending. I need you
to *know: I have loved*; I have love

but I do not have faith
that all our *good* will rid these times
of grit. I make *room* for when you *go*. I live
here in what will come.

NOVACANE

Alice is a girl of almosts. Like Autotune
the instance her boyfriend almost punches her
hurling his fist at the wall as she tries to exit
or the time she almost has a train run through her

in the forest by five crisp pairs of khaki slacks.
Alice is lucky. She recognizes rape
as a regulatory urge like birth control
or Manifest Destiny. She trades on the currency

of her own core value / that the opposite of EROS
is either VIDEOS or THANATOS. Sometimes she grits
when she smiles in the film reel. Whenever
a man shoots a camera across her autonomy

the room tilts foal red. By the time she gets
to Frank, she is addicted
to looking glasses & fingers
laced heavy around her trachea.

She spends time learning to protect her
teeth. Frankly, who hasn't been numbed by a life
time of violence. Alice reads her dental
school textbooks in the light by the bed. She

envisions her own agency. While they sleep, she sucks
the air between his lips & lungs. She says, "It's *super
-human* the way I can shut your eyes & still see
everything." She is trying to be / someone she wasn't.

SONGS 4 WOMEN

There ain't no love *songs*
for women. Only little boys

who shimmy out their father's
vintage, *harmonizing*

to wood-paneled living
rooms—one hand housed

around an invisible
mic or signing to the image

of their own abs on laptop
cameras (as evidenced

by DANCING TO
PONY ALONE

an entire Tumblr feed
of ostensible melancholy).

They *slow dance* to half
-opened tubs of Vaseline

the rehearsed vinyl of ponytails
halter tops & tight jeans. And

sometimes young ladies
get mentioned in the liner

notes of their lungs like all boys
are Icarus: lost sons crooning

to the lyric of their own self-
destruction. "There ain't

no love *songs for women*," I say
"only you.   But"

I lament to the most popular
pronoun in Top 40 music

"as is often true
of the second-person, you

can't decide." *Fair enough.*
I am a catalogue

of heartbreak's admission. I write
my own verse. I switch

the carpet shag from beige
to brindle in the voice

-over; *I sing la dah* alone
when our song comes on

I try not to get Rhythm
& Depressed.

LOVECRIMES

1. **Ocean's Eleven**: I throw a fistful of French-cuffed shirts on the lawn of our Malibu home when you tell me you're headed out of town to pull a heist with eleven army buddies. You die. I let the Rat Pack line your coffin with Franklins at your funeral.

2. **Pretty Woman**: You let me butcher George Bernard Shaw at a dinner party.

3. **Forrest Gump:** You wear a linen suit. You tell the undoing of our love saga to every Savannah bus patron, a box of chocolates luring in each.

4. **ATL**: We meet at the skating rink. I kick all my crew out the El Camino to take you home. We pull up to a house that isn't yours so I won't find out your daddy is a venture capitalist.

5. **Rush Hour:** We show up at a restaurant making the same Michael Jackson impersonations. Businessmen mistake us for lovers.

6. **Showgirls:** Just to prove to me there is life after former-teen-actress you don't become a chorus girl; we hitchhike to Vegas, all the way cross.

7. **Reservoir Dogs**: I eat brunch while you misappropriate sexual references in the early Madonna catalog. I refer to you only as Mr.

8. **Runaway Bride:** I save you from a man who speaks in sports analogies; you present a pair of sneakers when you propose to me.

9. **The Matrix**: I ask you if I should question my career path as a 21st century hacker— ask you if I should clear my browser history—you just keep feeding me cookies.

10. **The Last Dragon**: Sho'nuff, you drag on the 'gun. I glow within you.

11. *Murder, She Wrote.*

12. **Casino**: We're both hustlers but, when we exit the Tangiers on our wedding day, I can't believe I'm conning you.

13. **2001: A Space Odyssey**: On a mission outer space, you mistake my desire to rescue you as a trip in my cognitive circuits. I cut your life support. We both lose oxygen.

14. **The Shining**: We relocate to Colorado, our kid keeps telling stories about us—the wrong way. You take an axe to his writer's block.

15. **Less Than Zero**: I'm a freshman in college when I drive back to Los Angeles from the East Coast to court you; I find you riding my best friend. I take him out for a long drive in the desert. He keels over of heart... failure.

16. **Magnolia**: We spend most of our time watching child prodigy quiz shows in bed.

17. **Fear and Loathing in Las Vegas**: Ruminating on the loss of the American Dream, we shoot off into the Grand Canyon: Smith & Wesson.

18. **The Shawshank Redemption**: We build a tax shelter & a tunnel through "The Marriage of Figaro." I am sentenced to a life for a lover; I did not commit.

19. **The Royal Tenenbaums**: I wear too much mascara; I tell you I met my ex-husband in the ocean, counting the brand new stitches on your forearm. We only say I love you in a tent.

20. **Love Jones**: Late-nineties Nia Long: one turtleneck kiss drenched in rain & I quote a Sonia Sanchez renga at the lounge's open mic night.

21. **Eyes Wide Shut:** You make damned sure I am scared of masks.

22. **Ghost**: Ghosting.

THERE WILL BE TEARS

June 2015 & "Boys Don't Cry." They stand
as close to you as they can until you drown
in the spoor of their neck & armpit. Vapor
your lip's bow when they breathe. They live
for you in prisms. You either want
to kiss or sob. You take a step back
from the brick wall rising between your two
hands & make this moment more perfect
in your memory.   The Ocean
does not have the luxury of common-
place love songs. You must compete
with the ballad of whales, erode
into the tear ducts of mountains.

When your album doesn't drop
a vitriol of suburban teenage woe inundates
every net: bird, vine, & camera. Sad boys are
nothing new, but something about you
turns #hashtags into hearts
torn, turns heart—breaks into beat
& bone. I belt your songs in your car
full blast, a burn in my eyes;
like the only way to cry is to cover
my face, my eyes, to vibrato the cure
in someone else's lyric. In one song, you shed
more than I will ever remember. You channel
into tributaries. Sometimes   the ocean
is Billy Ocean—my *dad*
my feet turned up to the ceiling so I can
know what it's like to dance.

Sometimes the Ocean is
Childish: selfies, confessions
a portrait unapologetic.

                              I forget the conceit;
that Narcissus carried his lips
to the lake & journeyed
his own deep beauty. He got lost
in the valley of his void, vast—if I've ever
loved a boy, how could I blame him?

DUST

To put the Devil out of place
     I quit writing:
what he can't read he can't take, sure as be. I'm nothing special.
Just a *book*
marked with the lit end of a match. I'm not too proud
to *burn* it all back, *I wish*   *I could*

But there's no erasing   past *the best advice I got—*

        I quit writing.
I turn   *to dust.*

Sometimes I hear the *library* of my loves *laughing*
at me. Everything I worship, I either disappear or destroy.

I'm *nothing*
special. Know
what you can't see, you can't take—my ink, my one truth
left.   *I wrote* everything we are.
I'm not too proud;

I'd take it all back
     in like the lit end of a match. I can't *erase*

the past, but leave no *ink* behind   (the *dust* I was
the *dust* I do
remains).

I return to the book & rip through *the pages*
with all my *ink.*

                                        I keep
writing.
I don't *put you. Out*
here, I find religion
is just *the best advice I got* over & over
                        —*the pages turn / to* prayer.

SWIM GOOD

My father never learned to *swim good* enough to keep
from drowning. The beach was a battle I knew he'd lose.
The water roaring him deaf of me.

There is nothing more hard than to watch
a grown man punch his fists through the *ocean*
flailing at the loam with is every gasp. I saw

my daddy drown every day. I could count the silence
in his submission to his bathwater, his face under
the faucet, a sip too long from his morning coffee. The lure

(*Don't die.*) much *bigger than* I could muster. Daddy
swam at the very lungs. Chest tethered
to the EKG, in *this suit* of him. *Heart* fluttered.

Every time he submerged, I would chorus
in the undertow *(Don't die. Don't die.)*. Every current
ebbing back what was left of the beach.

There is nothing more hard than to see
a grown man draw his fists at the ocean. Say
I hope you learn to *swim good*. My daddy never did.

AMERICAN WEDDING

'People always try
to find ways to keep
magic inside them'
the first boy
who took my *hand*
says three months after
my last.

                    A tiny diamond
toils down my ring
finger. A generation
littered in *tattoo*; I stay clear
of getting marked—too terrified
what may take
hold & possess me.
                    I don't wear
a veil but hear
the three-fold chord
when I *ballgown* down
the aisle. I was

                    very good
being at arranged, wonderful
with beginnings—like television
in *America*—I don't understand
why I'm given away.

                    In the end
I have *daydreams*
of a needle flood

with ink. I crush a fountain
pen: watch my sole
disperse into a deep *blue* Ocean.

hello, LONNY BREAUX

ACURA INTERGURL

Driving my car
I turn off
the A/C. I ask

"How'd you
make such a *fan*
out of me?"

LONNY

—for N.

Mr. Christopher Breaux, this is X calling
with a message from U.S. Bank. We would
like to inform you that a payment of $_____
for your [fast-paced foreign luxury vehicle]
is past due.

wait a minute.
who is this?

Hello, Mr. Breaux, this is X calling from US
Bank. Would you be willing to provide your
Social Security number so that I can
confirm your identity?

hold up.
hold up. hold up.
how did you get this
number?

Mr. Breaux, I am a representative from U.S.
Bank. We are calling to confirm you are the
owner of a [fast-paced foreign luxury vehicle]
for which we are awaiting payment. Would
you be willing to provide your—

wait.
do you know
who I am?

Sir, according to my records I am speaking
with—

                                    **i'm motherfuckin
frank ocean.**

Thank you Mr. ...Ocean. Would you be
willing to confirm your Social Security
number?

                                    **did you? hold up.
lemme speak
to your manager.**

Mr. Br—Ocean... I can transfer you. Please
hold.

                                    [   ]

Hello, Christopher. Glad to have you on the
phone! I have X on the line and would be
happy to help X your concerns. Can we start
by confirming your identity?

                                          yea.

                                    **i'm motherfuckin
frank ocean.**

Mr. Breaux, I'm not sure what that means.

google me.

—beat—

Mr. Br—Ocean, I don't think—

Mr. Breaux, I am Googling you right now. You do appear to be… Frank Ocean. *Just tell me.* Are *you ready* to give me your Social Security number?

(*you ready?*)

OLD TERROR
After Henry Louis Gates, Jr. & Wallace Stevens

I
Against the wall, the car, the flashlight
his limbs did spread like a cephalopod & he knew
he was a black man.

II
This is a gun.
This is only a gun: Little Black Man.
little black fist.

III
Even in mosquito August
he is a suit. The black man
is always a suit.

IV
The black man doesn't mind
the frayed anger
blaring bass between his eardrums.
He just hopes
no one whistles "nigger"
after him.

V
The car defrosting ice
from the window glass,
not unlike a body drawn in chalk, the absence
of a man, or soon after. Even in the mist
they are trying to make black men
ghosts.

VI
Thirteen Ways of Looking at a Black
Power.
Ranger.

VII
"We invented the alphabet." he says
"And Algebra." But when his son asks
who invented the black man, the black man
asks, "Which one?"

VIII
The black man blooms, the body
a fruit inescapable—its provocation either
too ripe
or
to rot.

IX
Sometimes he leaves. To a child
any man exiting the threshold
of a door always looks
black.

X
There are only three words
written on the road
for Robert Johnson—
                          "God, the Devil…"

XI
This time
when the old prude pinches
her handbag in the elevator, the black man
turns, shows her his perfect
teeth.

XII
There is a movement. A black man
is always
involved.

XIII
The record skips—its forgotten
melodic fades into static. No one
stops to flip the black man back
to music. The silence
just keeps breaking.

SCARED OF BEAUTIFUL

*The look in his eye said he was imagining what it might be like to be in
another place—perhaps what it might be like to be another person, a person
people didn't need.*
　　　　　　　—Hanif Willis-Abdurraqib

How blue is The Ocean: blue as the word
we did not know we did not notice, blue

as the reflection that rains through sea
& heaven, as the scent of dye on a figure
upon one's own, its beatific sex
petulant as the fat of honey—water
the dye that drowns: deep red. How

blue is the ocean when we do not see
the Ocean: when The Ocean is no longer

a land we need. We know that
water is a lonely place—no real
distinction between odyssey
& abandon. We trek the wine
-dark sea, & parse between the taste
of a wave we know & a pain we can't

articulate. How blue is the ocean when we
cannot see blue: so caught in the chrysalis

of our own tongues we have not formed
a distinction between what is spectacle
& what is shadow—dispersing into nothing

altogether, the void of how we yet
see ourselves.

　　　　　How blue is The Ocean
when it is the only way of mentioning
our own abandon?

　　　　　Somewhere there is
a boy whispering into the shroud of himself
an echo he pulls from the gulf of his throat
like a seahorse; the lie of laughter.
He asks, "How blue was

　　　　　The Ocean
when we did not know The Ocean at all:
only salt & silt, their colors imaginary: like birds
that jolt pall lightning through the sky?"

TIME MACHINE

Sammy Davis Jr. Jr.
is the name of my dog. Yes
this comes from another book. Yes
I call him this because he
reminds me of a spry black Jew.
Yes, this is still racist. Even
as I say it to you the IST

wags out from both of us like a feist
turned loose. It wears the low-slung
onomatopoetic operatic
of tire swing hung from my neighbor's
tree—IST—a red cable fashioned
as a noose. The revisionist.
The southern transcendentalist.

They will use the same knot come
Halloween (the death man bringeth)
clinging to effigies of
tissue ghosts & come spring, garbage
bags clad in suits of papier mâche.
The satirist—(the ice man
taketh away)—a basketball

coach strung lilted & impeached.
The arborist: what front
yard isn't missing something large
& black & fearful hanging from
a beech? An IST in each as the
sonic historicist: the sound
wearing wind in its teeth. Gap-toothed

warden, sneer-sucking tongue
—and that was just the Disney version.
Even now, I may only hear
"Kin-TUCK-ah," but I will still see
Emmet Till & nimble Sammy
Davis Jr. [Sr.] in the
golden Cadillac to Kim

Novak's hiding in the backseat.
They file by the Volvo
window, parked at the Winn-Dixie.
My adolescent panegyrist
smudges the film, scans the white sheet
—the conic iconic—a
family of four in rain-spit grit.

I say, "Mom, it's the Klan." She looks
through the rear view, sucks Maybelline
off her teeth before scrounging her
purse for bills. "Well, you better
hurry on in there, then. You
better get on. Those eggs won't
buy themselves."

I MISS YOU

Pablo asks me when
I first knew *I* loved
the ocean.

He & *I* watch
the waves at Hermosa
ululate into grander versions
of themselves until a wall
reaches heaven like
rafters.

I fell in love
the first time you took me
snorkeling. (*I* want to say
I saw the metaphor
but *I* can't.)

I got so lost
in the corral
of my own breath
I could not *feel*
the riptide carry
me deep amidst
the estuary.

You
grabbed my ankle
pulled me in with the force
of both your arms. *I*
could have died
then. *I* could have died
right then—

the ocean
receding from my nose

& eyelids—your heart
flashing into me.
When a wave   breaks, there are
three means of encounter:
face the water head on, let
it bawl you *like* a car
crash; swim *away* fast
as you can; succumb.

the ocean is ENDLESS

                              Twice you told me I was
a whale, a heart as big
as the ocean.

In Foucault's "Panopticon," the philosopher describes an 18th century precursor to the modern prison—a tower manned by a watchman, surrounded by a circular corridor of cells. Although it is impossible for a single figure to watch all cells at once, so powerful is the mind's ability to project consequence, a prisoner will modify behavior to fit the psychological confines of a space.

In the myth of Argos, Argus Panoptes was an all-seeing guardian—the body of a giant, stalwart, tower—dressed in so many oculi it was impossible for all of him to sleep at once.

In our mythology, the reign of the panoptic giant prevails. Is it nearly impossible for a body to go through a moment without response to a hundred eyes, to image & meme, to snap, tweet, & flutter each instant.

The danger of existing in the tower of a multi-eyed giant is how little we see when we expect we are looking at everything. With one hundred eyes, we assume what happens in our periphery does not exist.

The Internet did not predict the release of a Frank Ocean album on Thursday, August 18th, 2016. The all-seeing eye did not foresee this release to be the visual album, Endless.

The scene begins in near silence. Frank Ocean sits on a workbench, removing a pair of gloves. A second Ocean emerges, an unnerving echo of the caption at the bottom of Frank Ocean's 2015 Boys Don't Cry Tumblr post ("I got two versions. I got twoooo versions."). The footage cuts to reveal the many-eyed boombox a Frank Ocean tunes in the corner while the other Frank Ocean fiddles with his hands.

His voice supine, he ablates the lyrics of an Isley cover to a love letter for critics & fans, asking us to examine the years spent in anticipation of this moment, our belief that Frank Ocean's new album did not exist.

In fact, Frank Ocean has always been imaginary—a character, a projection—the stage name of Christopher "Lonny" Breaux, a Louisiana native who takes on the title of Ocean soon after the ocean erases the homes of his family & loved ones, like a wolf sucking meat from its teeth.

In the span of time since Breaux's first album, Frank Ocean has taken the time to materialize, legally changing his moniker from his birth name to his synonym.

Adaptation after adaptation, the first five minutes of "Endless," Frank Ocean offers a response to years of panoptic speculation & ridicule. One Ocean gracefully drives plywood through a table saw. Another Ocean checks his cellphone. The Ocean has been watching us. "Endless" calls technology to task for the anxiety its watchfulness puts upon creation while recognizing its significance in connecting artists to fans.

Look beyond your world, try and find a place for me, Ocean pleads in the closing verses of the Isley cover. Another Frank Ocean appears in the workshop. He rubs his hands together before donning a pair of safety goggles. Sparks fly in the face of the camera, cuts to Frank Ocean, a work of art.

Sometimes the dream destroys everyone but me. The gas masks & automatics—concealment of its violence. Even though you are gone, you take away everyone I love. You take my breath, the hard leather of your hands closing the folds of my neck, limp as a wrung word. The blur in your grip disappearing as what was my then-husband slaps awake my face. None of us last many mornings after that, the part of you coming back for me more than killing us both.

Killer whales keep their color for a reason. The camouflage of black & white—a consummation to conceal their shape underwater; what I look like on land, a mere refraction of the creature, how deep I am, a beast.

How could I tell you, the safety I held in the beauty of this body for thirty years, the quiet focus of its human form, how I closed it from the memory of you, the memory of a body I believe I'd never known, now nothing of itself?

                                        How come the ecstasy always

depresses me so?

                                        How come the ecstasy always

depresses me

                                                        always

                                        the ecstasy
                                            ecstasy

presses me

                            How

                                come the ecstasy

depresses
            me
                so?
                so?

                so

                                come the ecstasy

                                            always

depresses me

                            How come the ecstasy

                                            always

depresses me
                so?
                    ?
                    ?

In the glower of the giant, tower, Frank Ocean was almost a casualty. Since first mention of "Boys Don't Cry" & its expected July 2015 release date, the hundred-eyed Internet kept abuzz with speculative news of the Ocean's next move.

In the year that followed, Frank Ocean heightened anticipation with posts on his website & Tumblr page—a shot of "Boys Don't Cry" magazine, poignant condolences during the loss of Prince, responses to tragedies in Ferguson, Orlando, & a library due date card playfully referencing the album's purported release dates.

July 2016 progresses. The Internet inundates an ocean of expectation for the impending Frank Ocean album release, but the moment passes—& most of the next—but, a year past due, there was still no new album from The Ocean.

To witness "Endless," one must be as patient as Frank Ocean has been with his music.

Its songs are challenging & autobiographical; The Ocean's kind of truth-telling is a phenomenal turn when compared to most digital era music-making. Most of Ocean's contemporaries erect lucrative careers off bildungsroman early albums that taper into radio-ready sophomoric collections—pop hits with mere glimpses of personhood.

August 2016, Zeus sends the messenger god Hermes to kill the many-eyed giant, lulling its body to sleep with song before exacting an incisive slit to its throat.

We are up close in a loud bar & I tell you repeatedly that I will not be fucking you. That we will meet in no state adjacent to love. That I just stopped fucking your best friend; that I have been pretending to fuck your best friend for over a year when actually, all I really do is make

the grey sky less grey.

But you know that already.

Twice you told me the trouble with me & men is that they see my secret, hale & sinewy—how uncomplainingly I stretch out the pursuit.

But I know differently.

Up close, the largest things become the most imperceptible. At the tip of your nose, underwater, it is nearly impossible to tell the difference between a photo & a landscape.

The Panoptes may be mythic, but its gaze is myopic. In our haste to say something about Frank Ocean, we ignore how little we have to say about The Ocean, the boy we fell in love with in pieces.

Wooed by his musical intimacy, we felt a kinship with his unparalleled ability to weave a narrative frame around his adoration—for his family, his lovers, himself.

Although killer whales are sexually dimorphic, the still-burgeoning dorsal fin of the young bull can be mistaken for the slimmer, more sickle-shaped fin of the full-grown cow. A highly social animal that hunts in packs, it is not uncommon for full adult females to appear

just like boys *comme*
just like boys *comme* just
comme just like boys *comme*
just like boys *comme des*
comme des garçons comme
just like boys *comme des garçons*

In the city of Argos, Argus Panoptes the All-Seeing was also known as Argos—meaning, "bright."

In what ways do you only recognize yourself in homage? A flash on the ripple of a needle?

When did this occur to you—that you could either be rap or soul?

Let me rephrase that: do you think that the chain reaction was set off so that something could be created that could also set off a chain reaction of its own?

You love the lyric & the snare. I love a good nostalgia. Nostalgia that goes for a while. It's crazy when music gets so powerful.

It can still be technical & poetic. I know how the spirit moves you.

I know what chord makes me feel about Wednesday afternoon, 1983. The taste of your skin like the time I first noticed

music. I, love the lyric & the trap   set; when we think we move in circles

we move slow enough to record   player— sticky hand in sticky hand. Sweet

baby, if you let me, I could be a better jam.

I want to record everything we fuck. The system. The boundary between you, I

swirl my lips around like a curse in bed, a love letter to us both.

Perhaps I love your body because in drawing you toward it I bring you closer to how I think of myself:

an insignificance; a reverberation.   Not in the way I have been accustomed to thinking of a reflection as the portent sadness, but in the way I feel far too vast—the awe you feel when curved inside what you can't see—my fluke, my contoured heavy-heartedness.

There is indeed a close interrelation between the predominant Western conception of manhood & that of domination. The notion, originally from myth & fable, is that the summit of masculinity—the "   hero"—achieves his manhood first & foremost, by winning over the "beast."

I detect what parts of you seafloor, shoreline—in the ocean you can find anything that tremors, trembles, shakes.

Echolocation is the remarkably imperceptible method in which whales use their sensory ability to navigate, emitting sound in water.

Whistles, clicks, & deep, guttural groans.

Although echolocation is thought to be an important communication tool amongst these corporeal beings, scientists also believe it allows whales see three-dimensionally—their wavelength, a ripple that inhabits each surface.

"Boys Don't Cry" incited a media frenzy spurred on by our belief we needed more. It was as if, without Frank, we had run out of something to pull on top of us & crawl inside, like a giant, skin.

And this is why there will always be a God principle. When you get to the point where you can't explain anything, the human soul needs to find something because we can't accept not knowing.

In the quest to find Frank Ocean, the knowledge we truly sought was a better understanding of inner myth. Why do we want The Ocean, whose career has been so subtle & so brief, to put out new album?

What were we expecting to gain from one album's release?

Killer whales have evolved over the last 700,000 years. Scientist often classify their organizational affiliations into three distinct ethnicities: Resident, Transient, & Offshore.

According to DNA analysis, there is enough differentiation between killer whale clans to categorize them as completely separate species.

But reclassification remains fraught with debate—the communal distinctions indicative of killer whale differentiation, the subtlety in their markings, often imperceptible to the untrained eye;

killer whales of different subspecies are not known to hunt together, socialize, or interbreed.

Killer whales of different subspecies are not known to hunt together, socialize, or interbreed.

They do not speak the same language; there are even marked communication disparities between killer whales of the same region associated with separate pods.

These ubiquitous scientific observations act in stark contrast to the brutal history of killer whales in captivity.

The victims of a blatant commercial experiment, killer whales have been plucked from ethnic groups & shipped overseas, exploited for their capacity to perform as powerful, reasonably intelligent, beasts.

Forced into social groups that bear scant resemblance to their natural order, killer whales are bred indiscriminately as livestock. In situations where this husbandry does not yield offspring, whales are artificially inseminated.

Killer whale semen is colloquially referred to as "white gold."

Stud whales are trained to ejaculate on command, stimulated by amusement park trainers using cow vaginas, other males, or a trainer's gloved hands.

This process of involuntary copulation has led to a lack of diversity in the captive gene pool. The majority of killer whales conceived in these unions are miscarried or stillborn.

Despite the perception given in killer whale exhibitions that their life in confinement is enriching, care-free, happy, "gay," captive killer whales spend most of their lives in isolation & confinement. Captive killer whales develop physical pathologies: the collapse of the dorsal fin, increased incidents of aggressively erratic behavior.

Although killer whales have an average life expectancy of 60 years in the wild, 92% of captive killer whales do not live past the age of 25.

Frank Ocean's slow build coaxes his listeners to climax—through intimacy, not a rote manipulation of anatomy. His choice of film as a time-based medium through which to release is indicative of his sense of pace & pleasure. In "Endless'" 45 minutes & 51 seconds, we see more of Frank Ocean than we have ever witnessed before. He twins & triples over a body of music that is at once generous & unselfconscious. Ocean asks us to think about our legacy. In the midst of all we can record, what do we actually witness?

Twice you told me I was a whale. A heart. As deep as the Ocean. When did you realize I was an apex predator?

When did you recognize you were a scavenger, suckle to the knuckle & neck of what I capture.

(What is left of me?
I'm captured.) But fuck, I avoid

telling you what we did. The sweetness of the bed. The way you slide inside my navel; you slick & glisten when asked to.

By the time we slide into one another we didn't feel any differently—the space between us so wrought with what we had already eaten, consumed, rushed ourselves through—blood, shit, water.

I only make love to you once. I cannot call its doing accidental. A taste for flesh we both acquire, twinning itself into expression. Like what I saw in beauty shop mirrors—fidgeting my young hind in the too-tall stool, finding myself in infinity.

Is this what we think of when we fuck?

Why is it we so often find such sustained discussions of desire among people of color?

The digital yearning to be seen is an expression of our own solipsism; a belief in one's self apposite to the passing of time—precisely what makes the Panopticon so effective. In order to police ourselves, we must first come to the ontological conclusion that we are worth watching.

In this, the Panopticon as a larger cultural mechanism mirrors the way in which movement enters the realm of courtship.

Within Western social dance, participants perform in ritualistic acceptance of their mimicry & conformity. The order, cadence, & expectation of contemporary Western music, e.g. EDM, call to action a movement vocabulary that parallels patterns of socio-sexual control.

EDM braces its dancers to a metronome of Orwellian precision. Its rushes of excess, which appear unburdened & indulgent, are in fact an ingeniously regulated system of manipulation that blurs the boundaries between freedom & intensity. The music demands, leaving no room for introspection. By the time the beat drops, we are already in the grasp of an industrial baseline, the demand to work harder under the vice-grip of an eye-seeing drum. When we dance in the digital era, our attempts to keep pace are, at best, acts of contrition.

After all, what other reason to bring music to the machine than to make sure the masses can keep pace? To build the giant tower more accordingly?

In the rhetoric of possessive individualism, the ability to champion our own physical, emotional, & temporal struggle outside the parameters of expected performance is a revolutionary act in direct opposition with the heterosexual, née paternalistic, notion that we must produce as our only guaranteed means of survival.

The slowness attributed to black bodies in America, is a thinly-veiled accusation that black people lack the ability to keep up with national thought—a stillness that reflects foolishness.

But Frank Ocean's stillness fits the choreographed means of radical black resistance employed throughout our neo-liberal colonialism—his lateness, a strategy of endurance & subsistence. Consider speed itself a terrain of forced power. Keeping pace, an exercise in creating a more efficient subject.

In "Endless," the high-contrast woodshop is staged like an industrious version of heaven. Frank Ocean toils away, focused & apathetic, fabricating portions of a structure we cannot see until the video album is two-thirds done. Ocean's agnostic deployment of patience in the release of his latest album is a critique on expectation; how much ownership we may place on any one entity. All this time, while we were waiting for Frank Ocean, Frank Ocean was waiting on us.

The era of the digital panopticon keeps us prisoner to a life in which pace is placement, our greedy hunger for the next moment prevents us from digesting the last one; our longing to *rush* toward Frank Ocean's new album almost prevented us from hearing it.

Was our love queer? Was it unusual? Do I have the right to attribute strangeness to the pleasure of my body?

How do you discuss a love for oceans colliding in a carnage of possession? An us so rarefied—the placement of our sex beside one's sex—always a marvel. The transparency of desire at the moment of penetration,

the tendency to insist upon the innocence of our sex, all part of the complex process by which whiteness is rendered invisible, unremarkable in the presence of spectacularized blackness.

Our insistence on ownership is a way of reclaiming the power lost in our displacement. The ability to claim familial ties through more than calling 'hey, sister,' 'hey, brother'—a reconciliatory acknowledgement of what we do not know we do not know.

We rush past in structures built on pods—not pillars.

I liked *having you round.*

I liked having you in circles.

The act of your sex encountering my sex, of my sex entering your sex, a liberation that disrupts the racism in our own unconscious—that we were, could ever have been, will ever, will be one.

But deeper still, we rush to structures built on pillars, not pods. We, in this, know what we are not mentioning, that our 'father' could be 'hey, uncle'—could be, not exact. We find false pride in ourselves, adhering to imposed definitions, pretend we are not awed by the sadness of how we were once defined: as colonies. As sexed & wanton beasts. We search

for an even more imposed definition: what it means to be someone's someone; what it means to be someone else's someone else.

But what other choice have I known? Am I not adrift, justifying, each time I fuck, that I might become?

A confession I drive into art solely through the mechanism of my own *genius*.

Hey,
you.

With each iteration, you take on a different shape. You become a different color entirely. The scent of flashbulbs burnt in the bed of nails or wet eyelashes, the faintness of dirty clothes.

But that's just like the past, isn't it?

"Endless" climaxes as two Oceans converge to load the wooden structures built in previous scenes. The Oceans scrutinize our insatiable hunger for digital culture. Over sparse instrumentals, they sing of a world pacified by panoptic devices, a discursive view of our recreational madness.

All the while, two Oceans continue to construct on screen what we can not see until a spiral staircase reaches *back* to the sky.

How are we still looking for a flat life? A flat wife? A smaller conception of what it looks like to spill forth from decimation?

Now we think as we fuck. This nut might kill us. This kiss could turn us to stone.

But human beings are put on God's green earth for at least one reason: to consume & be taken up & consume other people.

Will I keep *love*?

Have you fixed your fascination with wolves? With hunger? With beasts not big enough for you to even fill myself?

A killer whale is not really a killer whale at all. Although many continue to use the term, the creature heralded within this misnomer is more closely related to dolphins.

Since the 1960s, "orca" has steadily gained traction in common vernacular.

Although the genus name *Orcinus* means "of the kingdom of the dead," or "belonging to Orcus," the word "orca" is euphemistically preferred by some to avoid the negative connotations of scientific solecism.

According to some scholars, the name "killer whale" is a misappropriate version of the 18th century Basque phrase, *asesina-ballenas*, which literally translates:

whale killer.

BLOND(e)

NIKES

RIP Trayvon. That nigga look
just like me. And yes, I recognize
this is a vulgar elegy.

Just as the President
who could only say, "If I had a son
he'd look like Trayvon"

instead of, "If I had a son
he'd look just like me." So often
the body is used

as a way to mediate chaos.
Just like the Statue of Liberty
looked "just like Trayvon"

but America couldn't not swim
under the body of a black girl
& still feel free. And yes

this is a vulgar elegy. I ask:
What is it in you, that they
don't want to look like you?

Remember one thing:
Remember one thing:

Rule #2:
There is nothing more frightening
than the amount of ignorance
that accumulates

from inert fact. The gap
between protect & what they choose
to protect

       —America.
Little children, I do not always
recognize the unrest
in your revelry.

The way you arm
yourselves in black
& white as if your eyes open
& close for the first time

like an international funeral
pyre. You ask
       America"
What color
will you fire
when you die?

Will you burst
in the palm radiant
as a fist full of sugar?

       How sweet
is that Justice
that holds a blind eye?
Will she weep

when there's nothing left of you
to keep?

Rule 3#:
I saw a photograph
of a man holding his son
in a shirt that read BLACK GUNS
MATTER. The media is alive
because someone else is
dead. And hell
not only *bitches*

want Nikes. We gotta keep ourselves
in *check.* Even I wanna lace myself
in a running that's real. You know
the running is real
even if you don't love the race

in America. We wear *Nikes*
even when we Converse
even if it's inverse:

Rule #1:
Get fly & drowned.
You know no Goddess
of Victory but

rock the swoosh
every day, trying to
open Heaven's Gate.

You've got *two versions*:

The one I lay to my chest
just so I can hear your heart beat.
& the one your heart beats.

PINK + WHITE

You know you the shit
when Beyoncé sings
hooks to your high
notes. Not just the rungs
but the time

zones. A Thermos full
of coffee *black*, a map
of all the places
we have kissed, road
signs to primal &
so *yellow*.

Nostalgia, set
the colors intersect
the trip we pave. We said
we'd turn the guide
on age, ness less.

(You'd finally get right.
We'd move out left.)
But we didn't. Now we are
getting any older. My eye
lashes, winds to *white* to
crease the long line distance

with a smile—not quite.
Like I come clean
forget. The years apart
you. How much fantasy
has onced us. The atlas

we imagined. How *pink*
the light our hands spun
to each other. I know it:
just the blood steering
space travails more openly.
I know. It's only blood.

SOLO

"Do you love me?" like *Dirty Dancing*
don't call me 'Baby' I'm in the corner
by myself—with my cellphone, heels
gone jagged. I lose my temper & go it *solo*.

I'm too *loud in public*, four gins in
I can barely *function* make my move
'cuz the *timing's perfect*. Alto your earlobe
try to crank out some sultry
vibe for *you*. & upchuck all over my *"solo."*

I stay clear of white lightning—good
girl hour in ironic glasses, hide out
with some smart fellow. But I'm redbone
he prefer yellow: light curls, loose bounce
that's cool. I read much better in *bed*—*solo*.

I just don't *act right*; wind-in-my-panties dance
night, full eye roll you run through—blow
me off for 'tryna cute'—Lyft alone at sunrise:
how could you go leaving me   so low?

I'm jucin reg'lar & sleepin right, yoga, four-mile
runs. Adulting, bad as fuck, wish
somebody would cross...
& *catch* me solo.

Dominoes & best friends, moths in my intestines
on-the-low, & I mean creep cuz I cannot let
them know, what this love costs—these rain checks
—your credit kills my soul. (There's no beat
without heart or break, *though*.)

Now, Love, you know, *I ain't so vicious.* I don't even
want *picket fences*: some *protest*, but no *picket
sign*, I just wanna line up wit ya.
Don't make me better off *solo*.

You say you'll *act right*, 'we'll meet at the function
tonight.' My best dress at the barbeque but it's
just me & no you, spill my cup & I damn near cry
feelin' crumpled, red, & SOLO™.

NIGHTS
for C.S.

like this we nickname
all the *bruhs*. Like Bapo
Fluff & Reggie Whats
Prez, The Impossible Negro.
Big Booty Clarence (whose
nickname was just 'Clarence')
or Paco—no relation.
We felt like summer
was gonna last. Forever. Dozens
of orange roses direct to our door
-step & freshly cut
fades, combing by Vespas
to help us load groceries or hand
-painted sketches of our high school year
book photo. And if our moms ever asked
'we don't know how that boy happened
to get our {block right; chaos; home
telephone number},' like we weren't up
in our rooms signing bootleg love
letters in Cherry Coke lip
balm & the slow grind
of our tears.   *Nights*

like this spin bees into honeysuckle
all soft buzz & earthy odes:
to every less-fresh prince. Like last
summer, when we dozed
next to Lonny on the sofa
of our late-flick-turned-make
-shift-sleepover. Like everything

we imagined, deciding not to kiss
closer as the screen glow
etched a memory of his face. We knew
we'd be next
a chance to finally hold
his knuckle in the stark of   Days

where the boys
all had nicknames
for us, like: Females & Nah
Girl! …Who? & Don't Be…
You-Such-A, & Alone. Pretty
Tina passing by by
morning, on Lonny's spokes
strands laughing like a string
quartet as his allegiance bleaches
to all our midnight
notes—that was all it took
for us to let go
the dream entirely; for the fantasy
to burn & well our eyes
like a dozen
discarded petals. Some   Days

the only way being a black girl feels
magic is that it isn't
real. Like we're always stuck
in the meet cute
of someone else's musical, like
we're Best Supporting

Actress. But who are we
kidding? This isn't our first
time around the {disco; cul-de-sac;
fire department}. We watch
them ride off in the sun
-set & retreat back to the night
of day. Blinds
closed, heads covered. Headphones.
A full stack of burned
CDs.

WHITE FERRARI

"The beautiful ones always smash the picture."
　　　—Prince

We *ride* the Gravitron. State Fair.　　Every summer
our *dilated eyes* pinned in the desperate hope

that weight is real.　　　　　　　　I cling to walls
afraid I'll fly apart completely.　　　You catapult

the restraints of time & G- Forces.　Back
to the Future, a gravity　　*familiar.*

I worry falling
　　　　is something for which I no longer

possess the capacity. I look at pictures of *white*
people & wonder what it feels like to

land.　　　　　　　　Have you ever felt like that?
Where

　　　the ocean is simply a place
you've been?　　　　　　　　Like being vapor

is a thing you can *vacat*
　　　　　　　　-ion from? We replace
photographs with flashcards.　　　　Love

watching people:　　　　heads on shoulders, hands
in hands.　　　　　　　It has been so long

since my delight has been a document—
Gran Tourismo.   We grew up

watching black men drive fast white
cars through cities of angels: Rodney   King.

O. J. Simpson.   Even our fathers
GTO.   We make

obsessions & amusements—
                    was this the future

we intended?   We defy
whatever keeps us down

has kept us heavy   & the *ride* never ends.
In the end, you just figure out how

to float.   Amidst the guardrails
You always thrilled me   —releasing from the safety.

Risking death   in small
dimensions   to drift   untethered from the past.

SEIGFRIED

I'm not brave. You should have seen how I learned
to swim, clinging to the back of Bridget
's braid as the chlorine covered my nasal
cavity, the long back of my lungs. Every tiny thing
a blur like the color scheme of most American
homes: Pacific
       Northwest. That summer
we learned to distinguish ourselves
through the shape of our bathing
suits in *swimming pools.* My *speckled*
face marked most for consumption.
I would never be a mer-
maid. I would always
have a fretful relationship
with the coast.
       A crab—one Valkyrie—her
pincer clenched tight around the cast
iron edge between life & ether
swim legs testing the void as they
arch & rouge. I say, "her"
because that's what I saw
once I lifted the carapace. The ocean of future
bodies swallowing
its womb like a harvest; those solar
flares that fought
alive, so different
from the others.
       Of course, when I say, 'Ocean'
I am thinking about myself—how every time
I approach she is never the same

woman. *The glimmer of God*
I once housed often leaves me. All my life
I have spent in the battle
above which I can barely
keep my head.

GODSPEED

I cannot move at *godspeed*.
I do not move in *God's* time.

I don't know why the ones that love
God always hurt me.

I heard: if you have faith
the size of a seed you can transport

mountains. How do you carry a heavy
heart, faith in the grain of a seven-pound

fist? I guess, that's just not *God's* will.
You cannot question *God's* way.

I don't know how
the torrent God dries oft deserts me.

Once: a man made
me & God said I was

perfect. What else would a man do
in the sight of Grace except destroy?

I heard: you walk in the truth
& the light

touches you. And the dark?
Pray*god*, did

it reach you too?
Does it get to you?

There is no progress; there is only the infinite possibilities of the present.
—Michelle Wright

FUTURA FREE

In heaven, the clouds slip
like the face of the Ocean

like the way before leaves
turn gold, they are green

the way before leaves
turn green, they are children

the way everything
vibrant succeeds. I hear

the future is femme | male.
Like God gave Adam back

his spine. He saw us naked
& uttered no poetry—just held

our flesh to his own & embraced
us as residents of time:

      in ocean
-ography, a corpse

takes two-hundred fifty million
years to return to the deep

sea completely. Submerged
to our chests, our cheeks, we still

spit & swallow the dead
matter—us enslaved

people. What does
it mean
to say we

encounter bodies
of water?

Make sure you speak up
  : *Okay*

Interviewer: *What's your name?*

Thunder.

Interviewer: *Yo, aye be quiet. What's your name? What do you do? What's your first memory?*

A dream I had about going to Disney World. I was two; all of Pooh Corner greeted me at the Magic Kingdom with balloons.

Interviewer: *What's the most amazing thing you've ever witnessed?*
A miracle happening.
You.

Interviewer: *Ha ha ha, alright, what three superpowers do you wish you had?*

 To have anyone I want drown
into me, if I willed it—to make what I want
materialize
from nothing—I can
(fly).

Interviewer: *Alright, what's your name?*

:*I wish I could sleep without being dead but sleep forever at the same time.*

Interviewer: *Yo what's your... stop, stop, stop*

 I can make you love me
without me
even knowing it. I wish
I could (fly).

Interviewer: *That's fucked up. Start over right now.*

You know, the original words for sex were 'mas' and 'femella.' It was 'male'
that was altered to look more like its counterpart. We often say "females" as a
deduction of the familiar, but we're just bad at derivatives.

It's not.

Interviewer: *Talents, got any secret talents?*

I can disappear. I can make you
disappear without a word; cut things
open
with my teeth.

Interviewer: *What's your name?*

Interviewer: *What do you do?*

What you do.
What you do & this.

Interviewer: *How far is a light year?*

How far is a light?

—Year.

Interviewer: *How far is a light year?*

How far is a light?

...year?

Liner Notes

channel(ed), ORANGE

THINKIN BOUT YOU
I SHALL PROVE TO BE / WHAT I SHALL PROVE TO BE...
Exodus 3:14
O Christopher/ O Francis-I-Have-Not felt
Christopher Edwin "Lonny" Breaux, Frank Ocean's given name, which he legally changed to Christopher Francis Ocean.

> Alex Young, "Frank Ocean
> Legally Changes His Name,"
> Consequence of Sound, Web
> (23 April 2015)

How do you mend a broken heart?
...
How does the rain stop?

> Al Green, "How Can You
> Mend a Broken Heart" (1970)

SUPER RICH KIDS
Revamps Tyler the Creator's verse on the *channel, ORANGE* album recording as an autobiographical sketch of Frank Ocean written in his persona. It contains details related to Ocean's early life culled from interviews and biographical sketches.

> "Frank Ocean
> Biography," *IMDb*, Web
> "Frank Ocean," *MTV*, Web
> (June 2015)
> "Frank Ocean," *Biography*,
> Web (20 December 2016)

PILOT JONES
Frank Ocean was one of the more fascinating and polarizing R&B artists of the 2010s. Born Christopher Edwin Breaux in Long Beach, California, he moved with his family to New Orleans, Louisiana at the age of five. The aspiring songwriter and singer had just moved into his dorm at the University of New Orleans when Hurricane Katrina hit. With his future underwater, Ocean immediately left the academic life behind and moved to Los Angeles to give music a shot.

David Jefferies & Andy
Kellman, "Frank Ocean |
Biography," *Billboard*, Web
(excerpted above)
DJ Digital, "Frank Ocean
Attended UL Lafayette In
The Fall of 2005, But
Somehow No One Really
Noticed," *Hot 107.9*, Web
(27 June 2013)

PYRAMIDS
The Jesus/ I know died on a pole

References the use of the Hebrew word "adonai" (my lord") and the
word Greek "stauros," 'usually translated to tree, pole, or stake' as the
New Testament 'device on which Jesus was executed.

Psalms 110
"Stauros," *Wikipedia*, Web (5
May 2014)

BAD RELIGION
Translates the Takbir, "Allahu Akbar," *God is great.*

ULTRA, nostalic

STREET FIGHTER
References characters present in 90's arcade video game, Street Fighter II.

NOVACANE (sic.)
Been tryna film pleasure with my eyes wide shut but it keeps on movin'
Frank Ocean

The protagonist Alice alludes to the song's reference to the Stanley
Kubrick film, E*yes Wide Shut.*

LOVECRIMES
A catalog of film allusions in Frank Ocean lyrics.

"Cataloging Frank Ocean's
Obsession with Film,"
Pitchfork, Web (1 December
2015)
"Frank Ocean's Movie
References," *Reddit*, Web (12
May 2016)

Frank Ocean credits the movie *Ocean's Eleven* as the source of his stage
name.

"Frank Ocean," *Wikipedia*,
Web (22 February 2015)

THERE WILL BE TEARS

Mr. Hudson "There Will Be Tears" (2009)

June 2015 & Boys Don't Cry
References the expected release date and name of Frank Ocean's second
full-length studio album.

to vibrato the cure/ in someone else's lyric

Anwen Crawford, "Frank
Ocean, The Cure, and Boys
Who Do Cry," *The New
Yorker*, Web (15 April 2015)

Billy Ocean—my dad/ turning my feet up to the ceiling

Misattribution: Lionel Richie,
"Dancing on the Ceiling"
(1986)

Sometimes the Ocean/ is Childish

"Billy Childish," *Wikipedia*,
Web (16 April 2015)

DUST
(the dust I do/ the dust I was/ remains).
Genesis 3:19

AMERICAN WEDDING
Jesus Christ, don't break my heart.

Frank Ocean

The Eagles, "Hotel California" (1976)
Ephesians 5: 25
Revelation 21: 2

hello, LONNY BREAUX

LONNY

"Even though his legal name at the time was Christopher Breaux (he later changed it to Christopher Francis Ocean), everyone knew him as "Lonny," and it's what most of his close friends and family still call him to this day."

DJ Digital, "Frank Ocean
Attended UL Lafayette In
The Fall of 2005, But
Somehow No One Really
Noticed," Hot 107.9, Web
(27 June 2013)

SCARED OF BEAUTIFUL

The look in his eye said he was imagining what it might be like to be in another place—perhaps what it might be like to be another person, a person people didn't need.

"Frank Ocean's Imaginary
Album" by Hanif Willis
Abdurraqib for MTV News
(8 August 2016)

the ocean is ENDLESS

An adaptation of "The Ocean is "Endless": Frank Ocean's new visual album is a heroic read on digital culture" originally published in *Salon* (19 August 2016).

In the liner notes for *Endless*, direct quotes from cited sources utilized within the body of the text are italicized.

[DEVICE CONTROL (INTRO)]

...a tower manned by a watchman, surrounded by a circular corridor of cells.

Michel Foucault,
"Panopticism," *Discipline &
Punish* (1975): 201-225

[AT YOUR BEST (YOU ARE LOVE)]

...the body of a giant, stalwart tower—dressed in so many oculi it was impossible for all of him to sleep at once.

"Argus Panoptes,"
greekmythology.com, Web (2
February 2017)
"Argus Panoptes," *Wikipedia*,
Web (10 May 2017)

("I got two versions. I got twoooo versions.")

frankocean.tumblr.com, Web
(6 April 2015)

His voice supine, he ablates the lyrics to an Isley cover

Frank Ocean, "At Your Best"
(2016)

...legally changing his moniker from his birth name to his synonym.

Alex Young, "Frank Ocean
Legally Changes His Name,"
Consequence of Sound, Web
(23 April 2015)

[ALABAMA]

Sometimes the dream destroys everyone but me.

Duplex in New Orleans east
I was writing out everything, things I would tell nobody
Some things I didn't even tell me
Sleeping on my back, my body would wake up after me

Frank Ocean, "Alabama"
(2016)

How could I tell you, the safety I held in the beauty of this body for thirty years… now nothing of itself?

What could I do to know you better than I do now?
What can I do to love you more than I do now?

Frank Ocean, "Alabama"
(2016)

…poignant condolences during the loss of Prince…

frankocean.tumblr.com, Web
(21 April 16)

…Ferguson…

frankocean.tumblr.com, Web
(15 August 2014)

…Orlando…

frankocean.tumblr.com, Web
(21 June 2016)

…a library due date card referencing the album's purported release dates…

blonded.co, Web (21 June
2016)

How come the ecstasy always depresses me so
Chemically I don't have no more new places to go

Frank Ocean, "My Random,"
frankocean.tumblr.com, Web
(28 April 14) [italics added]

[U-N-I-T-Y]

Whoever held you down
Whoever propped you up
Built the structures with you

Frank Ocean,
"U-N-I-T-Y" (2016)

[AMBIENCE 001: IN A CERTAIN WAY]
"'Cause you are beautiful and you are young / You deserve to have the best in life"

This is an excerpt from the 1968 film "The Queen," the sample starts around 2:13. The Fader noted this as paying homage to drag, particularly ball, culture legend Crystal LaBeija, founder and leading mother of House LaBeija, who is the one heard speaking.

> "Ambience 001: In a Certain Way," *Genius.com*, Web (15 September 2016)

[COMME DES GARÇONS]

Although killer whales are sexually dimorphic, the still-burgeoning dorsal fin of the young bull can be mistaken for the slimmer, more sickle-shaped fin of the full-grown cow.

> "Killer whale (Orcinus orca)," *NOAA Fisheries*, Web (January 2017)

[AMBIENCE 002: HONEYBABY]

> "Argus Panoptes," *Wikipedia*, Web (10 May 2017)

[WITHER]

Let me rephrase that: do you think that the chain reaction was set off so that something could be created that could also set off a chain reaction of its own?

...

I love a good nostalgia. Nostalgia that goes for a while. It's crazy when music gets so powerful.

...

It can still be technical & poetic.

...

I know what chord makes me feel about Wednesday afternoon, 1983.

> Frank Ocean and Zing Zing Tseng, "Key Words: Paris, France," *Boys Don't Cry | Issue 1 | Album 3* (2016): 227

[HUBLOTS]

[IN HERE SOMEWHERE]

There is indeed a close interrelation between the predominant

Western conception of manhood and that of racial (and species) domination. The notion, originally from myth and fable, is that the summit of masculinity—the "white hero"—achieves his manhood first and foremost, by winning over the "dark beast."

Passage from *White Hero, Black Beast: Racism, Sexism and the Mask of Masculinity* by Paul Hoch (excerpted in text, provided here in its entirety for context).

Echolocation is the remarkably imperceptible method in which whales use their sensory ability to navigate, emitting sound in water.

Whistles, clicks, & deep, guttural groans.

Although echolocation is thought to be an important communication tool amongst these corporeal beings, scientists also believe it allows whales see three-dimensionally—their wavelength, a ripple that inhabits each surface.

"Whales, dolphins and sound," *Australian Government: Department of Environment and Energy,* Web (14 May 2017)

[SLIDE ON ME]
And this is why there will always be a God principle. When you get to the point where you can't explain anything, the human soul needs to find something because we can't accept not knowing.

Frank Ocean and Zing Zing Tseng, "Key Words: Paris, France," *Boys Don't Cry | Issue 1 | Album 3* (2016): 226

Killer whales have evolved over the last 700,000 years. …killer whales of different subspecies are not known to hunt together, socialize, or interbreed.

Hal Whitehead and Luke

Rendell, *The Cultural Lives of Whales and Dolphins,* University of Chicago Press (2014): 237
"Meet the Different Types of Orca," *us.whales.org,* Web (14 May 2017)

[SIDEWAYS]

The victims of a blatant commercial experiment… where this husbandry does not yield offspring, whales are artificially inseminated.

"The Fate of Captive Orcas," *us.whales.org,* Web (14 May 2017)

Killer whale semen is colloquially referred to as "white gold."

Stud whales are trained to ejaculate on command, stimulated by amusement park trainers using cow vaginas, other males, or a trainer's gloved hands.

This process of involuntary copulation has led to a lack of diversity in the captive gene pool.

"How Does SeaWorld Masturbate their Stud Killer Whales? Rocker Tommy Lee Says 'Cow Vaginas' And He Is Almost Right," *The Orca Project,* Web (9 December 2010)

…their life in confinement is enriching, care-free, happy, "gay"…

"My Old Kentucky Home: A Song with a Checkered Past," *Studio 360,* WNYC, Web (2 May 2014)

Although killer whales have an average life expectancy of 60 years in the wild, 92% of captive killer whales do not live past the age of 25.

"The Fate of Captive Orcas," us.whales.org, Web (14 May 2017)

He twins and triples over a body of music that is at once generous and unselfconscious.

"…the plural aspects and manifestations of the world, from its vastness to its multitude of worms."

Hilton Als, "Tristes Tropiques," *White Girls*, McSweeney's (2013): 10

[FLORIDA]

[DEATHWISH ASR]

…twinning itself to expression.

"We are not lovers. It's almost as if I dreamed him, my lovely twin, the same as me…"

Hilton Als, "Tristes Tropiques," *White Girls*, McSweeney's (2013): 10

Is this what we think of when we fuck?
Why is it we so often find such sustained discussions of desire among people of color?

Robert Reid-Pharr and Samuel R. Delany, "Dinge," *Black Gay Man* (2001): 85

The order, cadence, and expectation of contemporary Western music, e.g. EDM … By the time the beat drops, we are already in the grasp of an industrial baseline.

Kemi Adeyemi, "The Slowness," Newspace Center for Photography (26 January 2017)

… a revolutionary act in direct opposition with the heterosexual, née paternalistic, notion that we must produce as our only guaranteed means of survival.

It's about putting the white guy on the side of the intellect and putting the black guy on the side on intuitive primitive things. 'Oh, his language swings!' (snaps fingers.) 'It's close to dance!' Close to the animals, to nature!'

> Frank Ocean and Zing Zing
> Tseng, "Key Words: Paris,
> France," *Boys Don't Cry* |
> *Issue 1* | *Album 3* (2016): 226

The slowness attributed to black bodies in America, is a thinly-veiled accusation that black people lack the ability to keep up with national thought—a stillness that reflects foolishness.

> Kemi Adeyemi, "The
> Slowness," Newspace Center
> for Photography (26 January
> 2017)

…his lateness, a strategy of endurance and subsistence.

> Saidiya Hartman, "The Belly
> of the World: A Note on
> Black Women's Labors,"
> *Souls 18* | No. 1: 166-173

Frank Ocean toils away, focused and apathetic, fabricating portions of a structure we can not see until the video album is two-thirds done.

> 'I know there was a huge wait on this for all this to
> come out. I think it's testament to the reality that
> things made by hand take time. We're living in an
> age of non-handmade things. The iPhone is the best-
> made thing there is, but there's no evidence of a
> human being involved with it. Frank's music, which
> is very personal and literally has his voice, in the same
> way that all musicians have their voice, it simply
> takes time. And when you see the video, you see him
> building a stairway to heaven in real time. The 40-
> minute version is edited, but there's something like a
> 140-hour version. That's the whole thing. That
> exists, that's the art piece.'

> Marc Hogan, "Tom Sachs

**The era of the digital panopticon keeps us prisoner to a life in which
pace is placement, our greedy hunger for the next moment prevents
us from digesting the last one; our longing to rush toward Frank
Ocean's new album almost prevented us from hearing it.**
First time I was rushing for a wait
This time I'm waiting for a rush
...
Infatuation is a rush

Frank Ocean, "Rushes" (2016)

[RUSHES TO]

**Do I have the right to attribute strangeness to the pleasure of my
body?**
D. A. Carter
...the placement of our sex beside one's sex, always a marvel?

> Christophe Chassol: Is (sic) is the real word. It's the
> real word for the sex. My penis is my sex.
> Om'Mas Keith: You want to touch my sex?
> Christophe Chassol: When I speak with a French
> person, I say 'my sex hurts'. Yeah, for a woman or
> man, the vagina or penis is the sex.

Frank Ocean and Zing Zing
Tseng, "Key Words: Paris,
France," *Boys Don't Cry* |
Issue 1 | *Album 3* (2016): 230

*The tendency to insist upon the innocence of our sex, the transparency
of desire at the moment of penetration, is itself part of the complex
ideological process by which whiteness is rendered invisible,
unremarkable in the presence of spectacularized blackness*

Robert Reid-Pharr and
Samuel R. Delany, "Dinge,"
Black Gay Man (2001): 88-9
(Structure modified in in-line
citation.)

Our innocence … We search…

> Hortense J. Spillers,
> "Mama's Baby, Papa's
> Maybe: An American
> Grammar Book," *Diacritics*
> Vol. 17 No. 2 (1987): 65-81

You become *a different color entirely.*

> HOLOGRAM LAME
> when he looks at me
> in the light i am a different color
> entirely

> Raena Shirali, "I Wrap
> Myself in Gold," *Gilt* (2017)

…insatiable hunger for digital culture.
> Zing Tsejeng (sic): My friend has this theory that people who
> were brought up without the internet make better lovers.

> Frank Ocean and Zing Zing
> Tseng, "Key Words: Paris,
> France," *Boys Don't Cry* |
> *Issue 1* | Album 3 (2016): 229

***But human beings are put on God's green earth for at least one
reason: to consume and be taken up and consume other people.***

> Hilton Als, "Tristes
> Tropiques," *White Girls*,
> McSweeney's (2013): 86

[HIGGS]
**Although the genus name *Orcinus* means "of the kingdom of the
dead"…**

> "Killer Whales. Scientific
> Classification,"
> Seaworld.org, Web (23

...or "belonging to Orcus"...

Ken Olsen "Orcas on the
Edge—Killer: It's a Name,
Not an Accusation," *National
Wildlife Federation*, Web
(10 January 2006)

According to some scholars, the name killer whale is a misappropriate version of the 18th century Basque phrase, *asesina-ballenas*, which literally translates: whale killer.

Laura Klappenbach, "Orca—
Orcinus Orca," *About.com*,
Web (23 October 2013)

— Oeuvre Ends —
[DEVICE CONTROL (OUTRO)]

BLOND(e)

NIKES

Just as the President / who could only say "If I had a son / he'd look like Trayvon" // Instead of "If I had a son / he'd look just like me"

President Barack Obama,
"Remarks by the President on
Trayvon Martin,"
The White House, Office of
the Press Secretary (19 July
2013)

**So often, the body is used // as a way to mediate chaos.
There is nothing more frightening / than the amount of ignorance that / accumulates from inert fact.**
The poem *Nikes* makes multiple allusions to "The Dynamo and the Virgin" from the autobiography, *The Education of Henry Adams* (1900).

You may know no Goddess / of Victory but // rock the swoosh / every day, trying to / open Heaven's Gate.
Right around the 2:13 mark of the "Nikes" video,

Frank can be seen lying among some thoroughly partied-out debauchees on a cot with a purple sheet on him sporting the same Nikes that Heaven's Gate wore. The Heaven's Gate reference adds a particularly strong comment to a song that already takes a swipe at consumerism, making an implicit comparison between a suicidal cult's ideology and a life of vain pleasure seeking.

...

As a believer, Frank's trying to square his personal faith with others' experience of a divine voice, which can be used to justify violence. The voice of Frank's God seems to be his own conscience and his own best self, but he wonders whether "the indoctrinated," like someone in a cult, might hear someone else's voice as the ultimate authority. Frank clearly differentiates his own type of intimate, humane religious devotion from blind, unthinking ideologies of fanatics—bad religion.

JOHNGANZ, "Frank Ocean's Nike References This Real-Life '90's Suicide Cult," *genius.com*, Web (22 August 2016)

SEIGFRIED

"Seigfried," the fifteenth track on Frank Ocean's *Blonde*, might be called a metaphysical break-up song. Based on the mention of "a speckled face," the song may be about male model Willy Cartier, who's rumored to have had a brief affair with Ocean. The hero Siegfried of Norse mythology is often depicted as a handsome man with long, flowing hair, much like Cartier.

"About 'Seigfried,'" *genius.com*, Web (13 August 2016)

…one Valkyrie…

In the Icelandic version of the legend, Brunhilde was a Valkyrie—a warrior maiden of the supreme god Odin. Because she was disobedient, Odin punished Brunhilde by causing her to fall into everlasting sleep surrounded by a wall of fire. The hero Sigurd crossed through the flames and woke the maiden with a kiss. They became engaged, but Sigurd left to continue his travels. Later, after receiving a magic potion to make him forget his love for Brunhilde, Sigurd married Gudrun (Kriemhild).

…

In the *Nibelungenlied*, the story was slightly different. Brunhilde declared that the man she would marry must be able to out-perform her in feats of strength and courage. Siegfried (Sigurd), disguised as Gunther (Gunnar), passed the test and won Brunhilde for Gunther. When she discovered the deception, she arranged for Siegfried to be killed. The German composer Richard Wagner based his opera cycle *The Ring of the Nibelung* on these legends.

"Brunhilde," *Myth Encyclopedia*, Web (13 May 2017)

GODSPEED

Once: a man made/ me & God said I was// perfect. What else would a man do/ in the sight of Grace except destroy?

Mia: 'Another thought on perfection. The only problem with her is that she is too perfect. She is bad in a way that entices, and good in a way that comforts. She is mischief but then she is the warmth of home. The dreams of the wild and dangerous but the memories of childhood and gladness. She is perfection. And when given something perfect, it is the nature of man to dedicate his mind to finding something wrong with it and then when he is able to find something wrong with it, he rejoices in his find, and sees only the flaw, becoming blind to everything else! And this is why man is never given anything that is perfect, because when given the imperfect and the ugly, man will dedicate his mind to finding what is good with the imperfect and upon finding one good thing with the extremely flawed, he will only see the one good thing, and no longer see everything else that is ugly. And so...man complains to God for having less than what he wants...but this is the only thing that man can handle. Man cannot handle what is perfect. It is the nature. It is the nature of the mortal to rejoice over the one thing that he can proudly say that he found on his own, with no help from another, whether it be a shadow in a perfect diamond, or a faint beautiful reflection in an extremely dull mirror.

Frank Ocean, "GODSPEED,"
Boys Don't Cry | Issue 1 |
Album 3 (2016): 52

FUTURA FREE

residence time
noun *technical*
the average length of time during which a substance, a portion of material, or an object is in a given location or condition, such as absorption or suspension.

You know, the original words for sex were 'mas' and 'femella.' ...

"What does the 'wo' in woman mean, what does the 'fe' in female mean and why does each word simply just add a prefix to the already existing word for a male?,"
Reddit, Web (13 April 2017)